SCHOLASTIC
LITERATURE GUIDE

Harry Potter
and the Goblet of Fire

by

J. K. Rowling

Scholastic Inc. grants teachers permission to photocopy the designated reproducible pages from this book for classroom use. No other part of this publication may be reproduced in whole or in part, or stored in a retrieval system, or transmitted in any form or by any means, electronic, mechanical, photocopying, recording, or otherwise, without written permission of the publisher. For information regarding permission, write to Scholastic Inc., 555 Broadway, New York, NY 10012.

Written by Linda Ward Beech
Cover design by Vincent Ceci and Jaime Lucero
Interior design by Grafica, Inc.
Original cover and interior design by Drew Hires
Interior illustrations by Mona Mark

This book is not affiliated with Warner Bros., J.K. Rowling, or any of their representatives.

Jacket cover from HARRY POTTER AND THE GOBLET OF FIRE by J.K. Rowling.
Published by Arthur A. Levine Books, an imprint of Scholastic Press.
Jacket art by Mary GrandPré. © 2000 by Scholastic Inc. Jacket design by Mary GrandPré and David Saylor.

ISBN 0-439-23194-9
Copyright © 2000 by Scholastic Inc.
All rights reserved.
Printed in the U.S.A.

Table of Contents

Before Reading the Book

SUMMARY

The story opens with a murder in the village of Little Hangleton. Two hundred miles away, Harry awakens from a bad dream at the Dursleys, his cloddish Muggle family; his scar is hurting. Soon after, Harry goes with the Weasleys and Hermione to the Quidditch World Cup. The exciting match is marred, however, by the mistreatment of some Muggles and the appearance of the Dark Mark, Voldemort's sign. At Hogwarts, Dumbledore announces that the Triwizard Tournament involving three champions from three schools of wizardry will take place during the year. The champions will be chosen by the Goblet of Fire. No one is more surprised than Harry when the goblet offers his name as a fourth contestant. During the school year, Harry and the other champions compete in three tasks: fighting dragons, rescuing hostages from merpeople, and getting through a magical maze. After helping each other through the tasks, Harry and the other Hogwarts champion, Cedric Diggory, agree to a tie. However, as they both touch the Triwizard Cup, they are pulled through space back to the cemetery in Little Hangleton and to a fatal showdown with Lord Voldemort.

CHARACTERS

People

Harry Potter . . . . main character
Lily and James Potter . . . . Harry's parents
Vernon and
Petunia Dursley . . . . Harry's uncle and aunt
Dudley Dursley . . . . Harry's cousin
Albus Dumbledore . . . . . headmaster of Hogwarts
Professor McGonagall . . . Transfiguration teacher
Voldemort . . . . Lord of Darkness
                              and Evil; a.k.a. Tom Riddle
Frank Bryce . . . . Riddles' gardener
Madam Pomfrey . . . . school nurse
Rubeus Hagrid . . . . Hogwarts groundskeeper
Ron Weasley . . . . Harry's close friend
Arthur and Molly Weasley . . . . Ron's parents
Percy, Fred, George,
Bill, Charlie Weasley . . . . Ron's brothers
Ginny Weasley . . . . Ron's sister
Neville Longbottom, Seamus
Finnigan, Dean Thomas . . . . Harry's friends
Mr. and Mrs. Frank
Longbottom . . . . Neville's parents
Hermione Granger . . . . Harry's close friend
Draco Malfoy . . . . Hogwarts bully
Mr. and Mrs. Lucius Malfoy . . . . Draco's parents
Crabbe and Goyle . . . . Malfoy's friends

Colin and Dennis Creevey, Parvati Patil,
Lavender Brown, Lee Jordan,
Alicia Spinnet, Katie Bell,
Angelina Johnson . . . . Gryffindor students
Ernie Macmillan,
Justin Finch-Fletchley . . . . . . Hufflepuff students
Professor Snape . . . . Potions teacher
Professor Sprout . . . . Herbology teacher
Professor Flitwick . . . . Charms teacher
Professor Binns . . . . History of Magic teacher
Professor Sinistra . . . . Astronomy teacher
Alastor (Mad-Eye)
Moody . . . . . . Defense Against Dark Arts teacher
Professor Grubbly-Plank . . . . . Substitute teacher
Mr. Argus Filch . . . . Hogwarts caretaker
Professor Trelawney . . . . Divination teacher
Cedric Diggory . . . . Hufflepuff champion
Mr. and Mrs. Amos Diggory . . . . Cedric's parents
Cho Chang, Padma Patil,
Roger Davies . . . . Ravenclaw students
Pansy Parkinson . . . . Slytherin student
Cornelius Fudge . . . . Minister of Magic
Stan Shunpike . . . . conductor of Knight Bus
Sirius Black . . . . Harry's godfather
Wormtail . . . . Peter Pettigrew
Dementors . . . . Azkaban guards

continued on next page

CHARACTERS (continued)

Rita Skeeter . . . . journalist at *Daily Prophet*
Madame Maxime . . . head of Beauxbatons School
Igor Karkaroff . . . . . head of Durmstrang School
Fleur Delacour . . . . Beauxbatons champion
Gabrielle Delacour . . . . Fleur's sister
Viktor Krum . . . . Durmstrang champion
Ludovic (Ludo) Bagman,
Bartemius (Barty) Crouch,
Bertha Jorkins . . . . Ministry of Magic wizards

Ghosts
Peeves, Nearly Headless Nick, Fat Friar, Bloody
Baron, Moaning Myrtle

Elves
Dobby . . . . free elf
Winky . . . . Mr. Crouch's house-elf

Animals
Hedwig . . . . Harry's owl
Nagini . . . . Voldemort's snake
Pigwidgeon (Pig) . . . . Ron's owl
Mrs. Norris . . . . Filch's cat
Fang . . . . Hagrid's dog
Errol . . . . Weasleys' owl
Trevor . . . . Neville's toad
Crookshanks . . . . Hermione's cat
Buckbeak . . . . hippogriff
Fawkes . . . . Dumbledore's phoenix

ABOUT THE AUTHOR

According to J. K. (Joanne Kathleen) Rowling, "Harry just sort of strolled into my head, on a train journey. He arrived very fully formed. It was as though I was meeting him for the first time." Perhaps it is no coincidence that Rowling and Harry share the same birthday, July 31!

When Rowling began writing her first book about Harry—in a café in Edinburgh, Scotland—she was on welfare with an infant daughter. Helped by a grant from the Scottish Arts Council, Rowling took five years to finish *Harry Potter and the Sorcerer's Stone*. During that time she was also planning the six sequels, one for each of Harry's years at Hogwarts. Rowling's Harry Potter books have earned her the British Book Awards Children's Book of the Year and the Smarties prize. *Harry Potter and the Goblet of Fire* is the fourth of these books and has already set many publishing records.

Rowling is a graduate of Exeter University and a former teacher. She lives with her daughter in Edinburgh. Her favorite holiday is Halloween, when she holds a big party for her friends and their children.

LITERATURE CONNECTIONS
Other books by J. K. Rowling:
• *Harry Potter and the Sorcerer's Stone*
• *Harry Potter and the Chamber of Secrets*
• *Harry Potter and the Prisoner of Azkaban*

VOCABULARY
Like many good writers, J. K. Rowling does not "write down" to her readers, but expect them to work at comprehending the words she uses. Provide students with three-inch square sticky notes. Each day give individual students a word from the following list. Tell students to use a magical spell or whatever other means they can think of (like looking in a dictionary) to learn the meaning of the words. Have students write their word and its definition on the sticky note and bring it to class. Display these on a Harry Potter bulletin board.

derelict	seethed	cavernous	mullioned
incoherently	travesty	pursed	tremulous
regime	imminent	diatribe	protruding
peevishly	sanctimoniously	incognito	tuffets
moor	hindrance	embargo	palpable
vestiges	blatant	discordant	feinting
incantation	bemused	sporadic	belladonna
unperturbed	chivvied	mayhem	celestial
baleful	nonentity	malevolently	vindictiveness
manifesto	regurgitated	alleviate	colluding
unctuous	derisive	sycophantically	antidote
scathingly	complacent	fiasco	wend
illicit	demise	preamble	sardonic
berserk	plinth	quizzical	retched
rudimentary	glutinous	solace	interrogation

THINKING ABOUT THEMES

Review the concept of themes with students. Explain that a theme is a central idea or message that an author conveys through the characters, plot, and setting. Point out that the theme of good overcoming evil is evident in the Harry Potter stories. Other themes that appear in the first three books include loyalty, courage, truth, and the power of love. Ask students to look for these themes as they read *Harry Potter and the Goblet of Fire*. Suggest that they also look for other themes such as jealousy, fame, romance, and politics. Still another theme that students should note is that of loss: Harry has a taste of loss when his friendship with Ron founders; he experiences a loss of innocence as he grows into young adulthood; he suffers the loss of a fellow student with whom he had developed a bond of respect and trust.

GETTING STARTED

Try the following strategies as you introduce the book to the class.

- Write the title, *Harry Potter and the Goblet of Fire*, on the chalkboard. Ask students what a goblet is. What is usually in a goblet? Have students find a goblet on the book cover. Is it what they expected?

- Write the following prompt on the chalkboard:

    "Good sportsmanship is . . ."

  Ask students to complete the statement. Suggest that they save their statements to compare them to examples of sportsmanship in *Harry Potter and the Goblet of Fire*.

- Read and discuss quotations from reviews of the book. For example:

    ". . . what makes the Potter books so popular is the radically simple fact that they're so good."

  Encourage students to find and bring in their own examples.

Exploring the Book

WHAT HAPPENS

The gardener Frank Bryce stumbles upon Wormtail and someone else in the deserted Riddle house. His subsequent death awakens Harry, miles away, with a pain in his scar. Harry writes to his godfather, Sirius, about the pain. Harry manages to escape the Dursleys when an invitation to attend the Quidditch World Cup arrives from the Weasley family. After the match, some wizards wearing hoods harass a Muggle family by levitating them. When a Dark Mark, Voldemort's sign, appears in the sky, a house-elf, Winky, is blamed by her master, Mr. Crouch. Harry learns that the hooded wizards are Death Eaters, followers of Voldemort who never went to prison. Fears abound that Voldemort is near. Harry and his friends return to Hogwarts for their fourth year. There they learn that their school will host the Triwizard Tournament. Champions will be chosen from Hogwarts and two other schools—Durmstrang and Beauxbatons—to compete. The students also meet the new Defense Against Dark Arts teacher, Mad-Eye Moody. Meanwhile, a journalist, Rita Skeeter, keeps writing inflammatory stories about the Ministry of Magic.

QUESTIONS TO TALK ABOUT

COMPREHENSION AND RECALL

1. Why does Molly Weasley's letter upset Uncle Vernon? (*She put stamps all over it since she's never used the regular post before; she refers to owls as the "normal way." Uncle Vernon is unnerved by the mention of magic.*)

2. Why is Harry so interested in Krum? (*He's a great Quidditch player and is the team Seeker, Harry's position.*)

3. What is the Dark Mark? (*Voldemort's sign*) What does it look like? (*floating skull with a serpent coming out of its mouth*) When do Voldemort and his followers use it? (*when they kill*)

4. Who are the wizards who make the Muggles levitate? (*Death Eaters—followers of Voldemort*) Why do they act this way? (*It's their idea of fun; they don't like those who aren't of their kind, such as Muggles.*) Why do they wear masks? (*It's scarier; they don't want to be recognized.*)

HIGHER-LEVEL THINKING SKILLS

5. How does Harry manipulate Uncle Vernon? (*He mentions Sirius. Uncle Vernon is afraid of him; doesn't know he's not a murderer.*)

6. Why might the Dursleys be justified in fearing the Weasleys? (*They arrive through the fireplace by Floo powder; Fred leaves an Engorgement Charm, in the form of toffee, which Dudley eats.*)

7. In what way are the Weasleys like most parents when it comes to their children's behavior? (*They worry about their performance in school, manners, sense of right and wrong, and their clothing and hairstyles.*)

8. The Triwizard Tournament was conceived in an effort to improve ties among young wizards and witches of different nationalities. What are some ways young

Muggles establish ties? (*Possible: clubs, sports, Internet, travel*)

9. What insect does the journalist Rita Skeeter's last name suggest? (*mosquito*) In what ways is she like one? (*She's a pest; she stings.*)

LITERARY ELEMENTS

10. Beginning: Why do you think the author begins the story with a chapter about mysterious deaths? (*It's a good way to involve readers.*)

11. Point of View: Hermione and Mr. Crouch have different ideas about the treatment of house elves. With whom do you agree? Why? (*Answers will vary. Students may side with Hermione; she is a major and commendable character in story.*)

PERSONAL RESPONSE

12. Which of the wizard ways of traveling—broomstick, Floo powder, apparating, Portkey, carpet—would you like to try? Why?

13. Large public events, such as the Quidditch World Cup, sometimes turn ugly. What do you think causes this negative behavior at recreational events?

14. Malfoy uses an offensive term, Mudblood, to address Hermione. How do you feel about people who do this? Why do you think they act this way? What would you say to Malfoy?

15. Which of the virtues—bravery of Gryffindor, cleverness of Ravenclaw, hard work of Hufflepuff, ambition of Slytherin—do you value most? Why?

CROSS-CURRICULAR ACTIVITIES

SOCIAL STUDIES: *Wizards Worldwide*

Have students locate on a globe or world map the following places mentioned in the story: Australia, Albania, Romania, Ireland, Peru, Bulgaria, Wales, Uganda, Scotland, Luxembourg, Transylvania, Norway, Brazil, Egypt. Remind students that Bulgaria and Ireland fly their national flags at the Quidditch match. Invite students to choose one country and research and draw its national flag.

ART: *Pleasing Posters*

Students with an artistic bent might enjoy designing posters for the Quidditch World Cup. Encourage them to incorporate material from the story in their designs.

ART: *Selling Souvenirs*

Students might work in groups to create catalogs of souvenirs sold at the Quidditch World Cup. They might start with those mentioned in the book, such as a dancing shamrock hat and Omnioculars, then add their own ideas.

WRITING: *Fanciful Feasts*

Have students write elaborate menus for a Hogwarts feast. As they read the book, students can compare their menus to the food served at some Hogwarts functions.

MUSIC: *Creative Campfire Songs*

Challenge students to make up songs that wizards might sing around a campfire. Students might write new lyrics for existing music. Be sure to invite your musicians to perform!

WHAT HAPPENS

In his Defense Against the Dark Arts class, Harry learns about the three Unforgivable Curses. One of them, *Avada Kedavra*, is the Killing Curse; Harry knows that this curse was used on his parents. Meanwhile, Hermione starts S-P-E-W (Society for the Promotion of Elfish Welfare) to help Winky and other house-elves. Harry is upset when he gets a message from Sirius saying he is flying north because of the rumors and signs. On the thirtieth of October, the students from Durmstrang and Beauxbatons arrive; one of them is Viktor Krum the Quidditch player. The rules of the Triwizard Tournament are explained. Only three students—one from each school—will compete and they must be 17 or older. Students wishing to compete must put their names in the Goblet of Fire which will choose the three names. Much to everyone's surprise, the goblet releases four names, including Harry's. Many people are suspicious about how his name got into the goblet, but Harry is most hurt that Ron doesn't believe him. At the Weighing of Wands Ceremony, Harry has an unpleasant interview with Rita Skeeter.

QUESTIONS TO TALK ABOUT

COMPREHENSION AND RECALL

1. Why is Moody's class uncomfortable for Harry? (*He is reminded of his parents' death by the* Avada Kedavra *Curse.*)

2. Why is Harry so astonished when his name is called to be in the tournament? (*He didn't put his name in the Goblet of Fire.*)

HIGHER-LEVEL THINKING SKILLS

3. In Moody's class, students learn about illegal wizard curses which are abuses of power. Beyond the book, what are some abuses of power that you know of? (*Answers will vary. Encourage students to cite items from the news.*)

4. Why is Harry so upset when he gets the note from Sirius saying he is coming north? (*Sirius is risking capture because of Harry.*)

5. What kind of entrance do the visitors from Beauxbatons and Durmstrang make? (*Noticeable; they arrive in unusual vehicles.*) How do entrances sometimes influence people? (*They are often the first and strongest impressions people have.*)

6. Why are the Imperius, Cruciatus, and *Avada Kedavra* called the Unforgivable Curses? (*They are inhumane—they take control of someone, torture, and kill people.*)

LITERARY ELEMENTS

7. Character: Why doesn't Ron believe Harry's claim that he did not put his name in the goblet? (*Ron is jealous; would have liked his own name entered, never gets as much attention as Harry; knows Harry was tempted to put his name in.*)

8. Character: Why won't Harry try to persuade Ron to talk to him? (*hurt feelings, pride, stubbornness*)

PERSONAL RESPONSE

9. Hermione founds S-P-E-W. Do you think people should take a stand on something even though it's not "cool" or is unpopular? Would you?

10. The Triwizard Tournament is a test of daring, powers of deduction, and the ability to cope with danger. How would you rate yourself on these qualities?

11. Do you think the other champions are justified in questioning Harry's participation in the tournament? Explain.

CROSS-CURRICULAR ACTIVITIES

CITIZENSHIP: *Wizard Welcome*

Point out that the students from Durmstrang and Beauxbatons are strangers to England and Hogwarts. Have students brainstorm ways for Hogwarts students to welcome foreign guests to their school. Possibilities include teaching them the Hogwarts handshake or cheer, or writing a special greeting. Then have students think of ways to welcome foreign guests to your school.

WRITING: *The Divination Standby*

Here's an assignment for reluctant writers. Have them reread the section beginning on page 221 in which Harry and Ron make predictions about their fate for Divination class. Then invite students to write funny predictions about themselves for a week.

ART: *Magnificent Mural*

Suggest that students paint a mural of the October thirtieth welcoming feast in the Great Hall. Remind students to consult the text before they make their sketches. Suggest that they also make a diagram to show the position of all characters they have included.

> **TEACHER TIP**
> You may wish to have students who are auditory learners listen to the story on audiotape.

WHAT HAPPENS

Harry is sick over the article that Rita Skeeter publishes about him in the *Daily Prophet*. Hagrid shows Harry four dragons that the champions will have to get past in the first task of the tournament. When Harry realizes that he, Krum, and Fleur all know about the dragons, he tells Cedric too. Sirius appears to Harry in the fireplace at Gryffindor and tells him that Karkaroff was a Death Eater who got released from Azkaban. Moody gives Harry the hint that his Quidditch flying will be useful in the tournament. For the first task Harry faces the Black Horntail dragon but uses his Firebolt to get by it. He and Krum tie for first place. Harry and Ron make up and Hermione weeps in relief. They have a happy reunion with the house-elf Dobby in the kitchen of Hogwarts, but find Winky in tears for her master, Mr. Crouch. Harry and Ron are less than enthusiastic when they learn they need dates for the upcoming Yule Ball. Harry finally gets up the nerve to ask Cho, but she is already going with Cedric Diggory. Ron insults Hermione by asking her at the last moment after Fleur turns him down. Harry and Ron end up going with the Patil sisters, Parvati and Padma.

QUESTIONS TO TALK ABOUT
COMPREHENSION AND RECALL

1. Why doesn't Harry like Rita Skeeter? (*She writes false things about him; she twists things.*)

2. How does Hermione show that she is a good friend to Harry? (*She believes him, helps him, tries to fix things with Ron for him, stands up for him.*)

HIGHER-LEVEL THINKING SKILLS

3. Why does Harry explode at Ron in the Gryffindor common room? (*Ron has interrupted his talk with Sirius just when he was going to find out how to overcome a dragon. Harry's resentment toward Ron has been building for some time.*) How does Harry feel when he and Ron are friends again? (*relieved, happy*)

4. What is the "unexpected task" referred to in the Chapter 22 title? (*getting dates for the Yule Ball*)

5. How would you describe Ron and Harry's social skills when it comes to dating? (*awkward, unsophisticated*)

6. Why don't Harry and Ron think about asking Hermione to the ball? (*She's their friend; she's very serious and studious; they don't think of her as a girl.*)

LITERARY ELEMENT

7. Motive: Why does Harry tell Cedric about the dragons? (*He thinks it isn't fair that all the other champions know and Cedric doesn't.*) What does this show about Harry? (*He's decent and has a sense of fair play.*)

8. What would be fun about wearing an Invisibility Cloak? What might be some drawbacks?

9. Moody gives Harry this advice: "Play to your strengths." What strengths do you have? How do you use them?

10. Is Hermione right to try to liberate the house-elves when they don't really want to be liberated and are happy as things stand? Explain your response.

CROSS-CURRICULAR ACTIVITIES

LANGUAGE ARTS: *Bonjour and More*
Direct students to Hagrid's greeting of "Bong-sewer" to Madame Maxime on the bottom of page 324, and mention that they will have to pardon his French. Then invite students to learn some common French phrases to share with the class. If any students are already fluent in French, have them teach the others.

LITERATURE: *Literary Dragons*
Point out that dragons often appear in fairy tales and other fanciful stories. Invite students to meet more dragons by discovering them in literature. Students might search for dragon stories in the library or on the Internet. One book they might enjoy is *My Father's Dragon* by Ruth Stiles Gannett.

ART: *Perky Puppets*
Suggest that interested students create Dobby and Winky puppets. These might be simple paper bag puppets, hand puppets, or more elaborate string puppets. Encourage students to plan a show featuring their house-elf puppets.

WRITING: *You're Invited*
Have students design and write appropriate invitations to the Hogwarts Yule Ball. Instruct students to include the date, time, dress code, place, and events. Encourage them to incorporate the themes of magic, the tournament, and the holidays.

TEACHER TIP

J. K. Rowling has said that Azkaban is "in the north of the North Sea." Have students find its approximate location on a map.

WHAT HAPPENS

Harry and Dobby exchange socks, Dobby's favorite clothes, at Christmas. At the Yule Ball, Harry and Ron are flabbergasted when Hermione turns up with Krum and are stunned by how pretty she looks. After one dance, the boys ignore their dates and take a walk in the garden. They overhear Hagrid telling Madame Maxime he is part giant. Cedric repays Harry for his help with the dragons by telling him to take a bath with his golden egg. In a nighttime encounter with Moody, Harry lends him the Marauder's Map. Harry is puzzled about why Moody has searched Snape's office. Harry desperately searches for a charm for his tournament challenge and is finally helped by Dobby, who gives him gillyweed so he can breathe underwater. After rescuing Ron from the merpeople, he waits to be sure the other champions appear for their hostages. Finally, he rescues Gabrielle; her sister Fleur was attacked by grindylows and couldn't finish the task. Although Harry exceeds the time limit, he gets extra points for moral fiber and ties with Cedric for first place.

QUESTIONS TO TALK ABOUT
COMPREHENSION AND RECALL

1. Why is Percy at the Yule Ball? (*He has been promoted and is a representative for Mr. Crouch.*)

2. What does Harry learn about giants from Ron? (*They're vicious; it's in their nature to kill; most have been done away with by Aurors.*) How does this differ from Hermione's point of view? (*She says the hysteria about them is bigotry; they aren't all like that.*)

3. Why does Cedric help Harry with the golden egg? (*Harry tipped him off about the dragons.*) Why is Harry reluctant to take his advice? (*He's sore that Cedric took Cho to the ball.*)

4. Why does Hagrid want Harry to win the tournament? (*to show that Dumbledore is right to let anyone into Hogwarts who can do magic, no matter what his or her background*)

5. How does Moaning Myrtle help Harry? (*She tells him to put the egg in the water; gives hints about merpeople.*)

6. How does Moody keep Snape from touching Harry under his Invisibility Cloak? (*He says he'll tell Dumbledore about Snape's interest in Harry, implying that Snape has it in for Harry.*)

HIGHER-LEVEL THINKING SKILLS

7. Why might Karkaroff not like Krum to be too friendly with Hermione? (*He might think that Krum will give away Durmstrang secrets.*)

8. Why does Harry wear Dobby's socks to the ball? (*He cares about Dobby's feelings.*)

9. Why is Ron so upset that Hermione is at the ball with Krum? (*Possible: He's jealous. He says she is fraternizing with the enemy.*)

10. Why does Harry agree to lend the Marauder's Map to Moody? (*He owes him a favor; he's glad Moody doesn't ask where he got it; he trusts Moody.*)

11. What does it show about Harry that he waits to see if the other champions find and rescue their hostages? (*He cares more about people than about winning. He's decent.*)

LITERARY ELEMENT

12. Foreshadowing: How was Harry's fall on the stairs foreshadowed earlier in the book? (*Neville tripped on the same trick step.*)

PERSONAL RESPONSE

13. Krum has trouble saying Hermione's name. How do you feel when people mispronounce your name? When is it okay? When isn't it?

14. Hagrid's dad tells him never to be ashamed of who he is. Why is this important advice?

CROSS-CURRICULAR ACTIVITIES

WRITING: *Crazy Creams*
Remind students that Fred and George make and sell a food called Canary Creams that causes the eater to burst into feathers. Challenge students to write a recipe for Canary Creams. They might also write an ad to promote these unusual treats.

SOCIAL STUDIES: *Happy Holiday*
Point out that on the day after Christmas, called Boxing Day, Harry and his friends slept late. Explain that in England, December 26 has traditionally been a day off for employees. The name Boxing Day derives from the fact that employers give a "Christmas box"—a payment or gift—to workers. Encourage students to find out more about Boxing Day, such as where else it is observed, when it got started, and any other traditions associated with it.

MUSIC: *Merry Melodies*
Students might enjoy making a tape of music that they think would be played at the Hogwarts Yule Ball.

DRAMA: *Gracious Living*
Recall with students how inept Harry and Ron are with their dates at the Yule Ball. Talk about why good manners can make a difference. Then invite volunteers to role-play good manners in different social situations. Possible scenarios might include introducing a friend to someone or asking someone to go out.

TEACHER TIP

If you're teaching how to write thank-you notes, give students this fun and challenging assignment: Have them pretend they are Harry and write a thank you to the Dursleys for their Christmas present!

WHAT HAPPENS

Harry and his friends meet Sirius at a cave near Hogsmeade. He tells them how Crouch's son was caught with Death Eaters and sentenced to Azkaban, where he died. They all wonder where Crouch is; he hasn't been seen in months. Back at school Hermione gets hate mail, Harry learns about the third task, and Mr. Crouch makes a strange appearance in which Krum is attacked. Harry has a frightening dream in Divination class and again wakes up with his scar hurting. In Dumbledore's office, Harry discovers the Pensieve, a repository for Dumbledore's excess thoughts. He learns more about those who gave evidence about Voldemort; Karkaroff and Bagman are among them. He also learns what happened to Neville Longbottom's parents and that Crouch's son was a suspect.

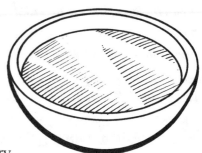

QUESTIONS TO TALK ABOUT

COMPREHENSION AND RECALL

1. How does Snape treat Harry? (*contemptuously; often unfairly; in a threatening way*)

2. What is an Animagus? (*someone who can turn into an animal*) What animal does Sirius become? (*a dog*)

3. What does Fudge suggest that Madame Maxime is? (*a giant*)

4. Why was Mr. Crouch's son tried by the Council? (*He was caught associating with supporters of Voldemort.*)

5. What does Dumbledore think it means when Harry's scar hurts? (*Voldemort is near or is feeling a strong surge of hate.*)

6. Why is Neville Longbottom being brought up by his grandmother? (*His parents became insane after being tortured by Lord Voldemort's supporters.*)

HIGHER-LEVEL THINKING SKILLS

7. How did Crouch become like those he was fighting against? (*He used violence; was ruthless and cruel.*)

8. In what way is Percy Weasley like his boss, Mr. Crouch? (*They're both sticklers for the rules. They don't see the human side of things.*)

9. Why does Krum compliment Harry on his flying after he learns that Harry and Hermione are just friends? (*He's relieved that there's nothing romantic between them; he was jealous.*)

10. Why is Hagrid so incensed at Karkaroff's behavior toward Dumbledore? (*Hagrid is very loyal; Karkaroff has gone beyond rudeness to insult by spitting and showing mistrust.*)

LITERARY ELEMENT

11. Mood: What mood does the author create when Harry slips into the scene in the Pensieve? (*frightening, cold, dark and serious*)

12. Dumbledore puts his excess thoughts into the Pensieve to sort them out. How do you sort out your thoughts?

13. The Council of Magical Law lets Ludo Bagman off because he was a popular Quidditch player for England. Do you think athletes or other well-known people should get special treatment? Why or why not?

CROSS-CURRICULAR ACTIVITIES

LANGUAGE ARTS: *Verb Magic*
Draw students' attention to J. K. Rowling's use of lively and exact verbs. Give examples such as:

> "Hermione hastily *rifled* through the magazine."

> ". . . he *clambered* through the portrait."

Ask students what verbs most people would use in place of the italicized words (*looked, climbed*). Then talk about how Rowling's use of language adds to the story. Conclude by asking students to keep a list of effective verbs as they read the rest of the book.

MATH: *Make a Maze*
Recall with students that the last task of the Triwizard Tournament involves a magical maze. Provide students with graph paper and challenge them to make their own intricate mazes. You might also want to relate this activity to the maze on the poster that accompanies this guide.

ART: *Zany Zoo*
Review some of the magical creatures that appear in the book. For example, the Blast-Ended Skrewts, four kinds of dragons, niflers, snakes, phoenix, owls, and unicorns. Suggest that students work in groups to create a pictorial Harry Potter zoo of magical creatures.

SCIENCE: *Hogwarts Weather Reports*
Read aloud the following passage: "As they entered March the weather became drier, but cruel winds skinned their hands and faces. . . " Then have students find other passages in the book that describe the season or weather. Ask students to write weather reports for different days at Hogwarts. Remind them to use centigrade readings, as is done in England.

TEACHER TIP

Write "Pensieve" on the chalkboard. Draw students' attention to the play on words the author uses. Ask: What does it mean when someone is pensive? What is a sieve?

WHAT HAPPENS

Harry practices learning his charms for the third task. He is touched that Mrs. Weasley and Bill show up to watch. Harry begins making his way through the maze. He hears Fleur scream; she is out. He finds Krum doing the Cruciatus Curse on Cedric and stops him. He meets a sphinx and figures out her riddle. Just as he is about to get the Triwizard Cup, he sees Cedric running toward it too. He saves Cedric from a gigantic spider and they both touch the cup together. Suddenly they are transported to the cemetery in Little Hangleton where Wormtail and Voldemort are waiting. Wormtail kills Cedric and ties Harry to a grave. Using dark magic, including some of Harry's blood, Voldemort rises again. His followers soon appear; one of them is Lucius Malfoy. Voldemort makes Harry duel, but their wands become connected by a golden thread. The ghosts of people Voldemort has killed come out of his wand. Two of them are Harry's parents. With their help, Harry manages to reach the Portkey and return to Hogwarts. There he learns that Crouch's son, not dead at all, has taken over the body of Moody and betrayed Harry to Voldemort. Fudge and Dumbledore argue about what actions to take in the future, and there is a parting of the ways. At the final dinner, Dumbledore toasts both Cedric and Harry. Of the dark times ahead, he says, "We are only as strong as we are united, as weak as we are divided." Harry returns to the Dursleys knowing he will have to face whatever comes.

QUESTIONS TO TALK ABOUT
COMPREHENSION AND RECALL

1. Why do Cedric and Harry touch the Triwizard Cup at the same time? (*They agree to do it together since they've helped each other in the maze. It's the fair and decent thing to do.*)

2. If Wormtail is so petrified of Voldemort, why does he help him rise again? (*The Death Eaters thrive on fear.*) How does Voldemort reward him? (*replaces the hand Wormtail cut off for him with a silver one*)

3. How does Voldemort treat his returned followers? (*He tortures those who didn't believe he would rise again.*)

4. What was the sacrifice that saved Harry from Voldemort as a child? (*his mother's love; she gave up her life for him*)

5. Why did Voldemort want Harry's blood in his rebirthing? (*for the protection Harry's mother gave him*)

6. What happened to the real Mad-Eye Moody? (*Crouch's son stunned him and controlled him, then used Polyjuice Potion to impersonate him.*)

7. Why did Rita stop writing for the *Daily Prophet*? (*Hermione found out her secret: She was an unregistered Animagus and was listening as a bug. Hermione captured her and put her in a jar.*)

HIGHER-LEVEL THINKING SKILLS

8. How does Harry's instinct to help others affect him during each tournament task? (*It causes him to level the playing field and to risk his own chances.*)

9. How does the Priori Incantatem spell help Harry? (*It causes the spells once* *performed by Voldemort's wand to regurgitate and brings up his parents and others killed by Voldemort. They give him time to get the Portkey.*)

10. Dumbledore says that Fudge is blinded by the power of his office. What does he mean? (*Fudge is so interested in power and rules that he is blind to the truth about Voldemort.*) Can you think of real-life situations in which this occurred?

11. What does "divide and conquer" mean? (*get people to fight among themselves instead of the enemy*) How might this apply to wizards in the future? (*Those who are against Voldemort have parted ways. This could make it easier for Voldemort to seize power.*)

12. What is the title of the last chapter? (*The Beginning*) In what way is the end of the book also a beginning? (*Voldemort is back; the wizards have split camps.*)

LITERARY ELEMENT

13. Mood: Why does the author have the third task take place at night? (*It creates a sense of mystery, darkness, and the unknown.*)

PERSONAL RESPONSE

14. The champions are exempted from exams. Do you think this is fair? Explain.

15. In competition, is winning all that matters? What do you think the author's point of view is? What is yours?

CROSS-CURRICULAR ACTIVITIES

SOCIAL STUDIES: *Scoops and Snoops*
Rita Skeeter, a new character in the Harry Potter books, raises some interesting questions about news and newspapers. Have the class review news articles in local and national papers. Have them identify the answers to the five W questions in a news article. Discuss the differences among news articles, features, editorials, columns, and so forth. Have students look for examples of slant, innuendo, and the citing of sources of information.

SPORTS: *The Real Thing*
Discuss with students Harry's approach to sports and his portrayal of sportsmanship. Then ask students to suggest real-life examples of athletes who practice good sportsmanship as opposed to just playing to win or for fame and money.

WRITING: *Real Riddles*
Have students reread the riddle the sphinx gives to Harry on page 629. Then challenge them to write similar riddles for classmates to answer.

ART: *Good Luck Greetings*
Classroom artists might enjoy making good luck cards for the participants in the Triwizard Tournament. Remind students to "wave their wands" and create magical effects with pop-ups, windows, accordion folds, and other clever devices.

TEACHER TIP

Just before a test, point out to students that Harry feels more confident as he faces the third task because he has prepared well for it.

Summarizing the Book

PUTTING IT ALL TOGETHER

Choose from these activities to help students review and summarize *Harry Potter and the Goblet of Fire.*

CLASS PROJECT: *Hogwarts Yearbook*

Have students create a yearbook for the Hogwarts School for Witchcraft and Wizardry. The class should first compile a list of the faculty and students who attend (see page 3 of this guide as a starting point). If your class has read the three earlier books, students may also wish to include characters that appear in them. Have students decide among themselves who will perform the following tasks: yearbook design, pictures of faculty and students, and the creation of text to accompany each entry. Challenge students to think of magical twists for this yearbook!

GROUP PROJECT: *Thinking It Over*

Ask students to identify the different themes in the book (see page 5 of this guide for suggestions) and to note quotations and passages that contain important messages. Give, as an example, this statement made by Dumbledore: "... it matters not what someone is born, but what they grow to be." Then hold a class discussion to examine the themes that students identify.

GROUP PROJECT: *Chapter Wizards*

Assign groups of students one chapter each to summarize for the class. Suggest that students present their summaries in various ways—acting out key events, using story maps, making lists of important scenes, rereading significant passages aloud, or creating pictorial time lines.

PARTNER PROJECT: *An Enchanted Year*

Ask students to work in pairs to make calendars for the Hogwarts school year. Tell students to include the different feasts and other celebrations, sporting events, exam periods, vacations, arrival and departure days on the Hogwarts train, and any other special days or occasions at the school. Suggest that students also make an illustration for each month.

INDIVIDUAL PROJECT: *Sneak-a-Peek Pictures*

Invite students to choose five dramatic scenes in the story to illustrate. Provide two large sheets of paper per student. Have students mark off five squares or rectangles for their pictures. Explain that these should be distributed on the page (see illustration).

After students complete their paintings or drawings, they should then place the second sheet of paper over the first and cut out flaps so that when they lift each flap, a picture is revealed. Students can then give talks on the book, displaying a picture as they come to that part of the story.

EVALUATION IDEAS
Provide a set of rubrics to use in assessing one or more of the summarizing projects. For example, a rubric for the Hogwarts Yearbook might include these objectives:
• Did students organize and design the yearbook well?
• Did students do a thorough and accurate job of including all the important teachers and students?
• Is the text well written?
• Did students create a yearbook that reflects the unusual nature of the school?

TEACHER TIP

As they review this book, students might also find new insights about it on Scholastic's Web site at http://teacher.scholastic.com.

Answers for Reproducibles
page 20: Quidditch—1. A team has seven players. 2. Possible: Players score goals with the Quaffle. The Seeker's job is to find and capture the Snitch. 3. long oval field with golden goal posts at either end. 4. Mascots perform: The veela dance and the leprechauns have a light show. 5. robes 6. Quaffle, Bludgers, Snitch, broomsticks
page 21: 4.–10. Answers will vary.
page 22: 1. d 2. e 3. a 4. h 5. g 6. c 7. j 8. k 9. i 10. b 11. l 12. f
page 23: Possible: 1. Stands up to Malfoy when he says mean things about Ron's mother. Page 204. 2. Mentions Sirius when he wants to go to Quidditch World Cup because he knows Uncle Vernon fears him. Page 33. 3. Plans his excursion to the prefects' bathroom to find out about golden egg. Page 458. 4. Is called to the Weighing of the Wands just as Snape is about to give him poison. Page 301. 5. Practices the Summoning Charm so he can summon his Firebolt for the first task of the tournament. Page 345. 6. Writes to Sirius. Page 291. 7. Uses a magic spell on Krum during the third task after Krum does the Cruciatus Curse on Cedric. Page 627.
page 24: Students' graphs may vary, but students should be able to defend their choices.
back cover: 1. Noise 2. Color 3. Fortunetelling 4. Size 5. Hateful and Horrible 6. Clothing 7. Unhappy 8. Movement 9. Food

Name: _____

Quazy Quidditch

Is Quidditch like your favorite sport in any way? Fill in the chart to compare the two sports.

	Quidditch	**Another Sport**
1. Number of Players		
2. Basic Rules		
3. Description of Playing Field		
4. Pre-Championship-Game Entertainment		
5. Uniforms		
6. Equipment		

20

Scholastic Literature Guide • *Harry Potter and the Goblet of Fire* © 2000 J.K. Rowling. All rights reserved.

Name: _____

Forbidden at Hogwarts

At the beginning of the term, students are reminded that it is against the rules to have certain things at school. Use your imagination to finish the list of items that are forbidden at Hogwarts. On the back of this page, draw a picture of one of the forbidden things.

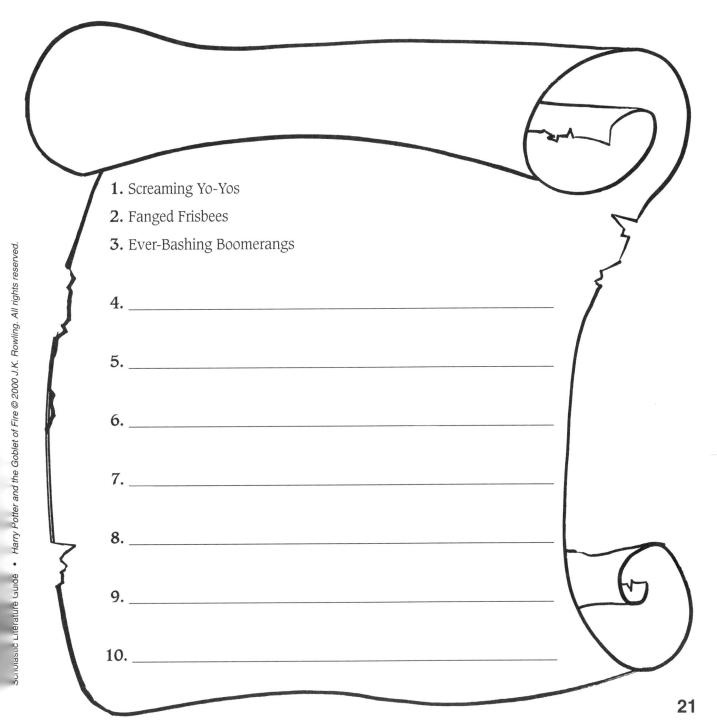

1. Screaming Yo-Yos

2. Fanged Frisbees

3. Ever-Bashing Boomerangs

4. _____

5. _____

6. _____

7. _____

8. _____

9. _____

10. _____

Scholastic Literature Guide • Harry Potter and the Goblet of Fire © 2000 J.K. Rowling. All rights reserved.

Learning English

Harry and his friends speak English, but they don't always use the same words Americans do. Match each word Harry uses to the one(s) you would say.

1. petrol

2. fortnight

3. biscuit

4. cuppa

5. dustbin

6. queue

7. galoshes

8. crisps

9. treacle

10. cutlery

11. bloke

12. mum

a. cookie

b. silverware

c. line

d. gas

e. two weeks

f. mother

g. garbage can

h. cup of tea

i. molasses

j. boots

k. potato chips

l. guy or chap

Scholastic Literature Guide • *Harry Potter and the Goblet of Fire* © 2000 J.K. Rowling. All rights reserved.

Name: _____

How Harry Does It

Harry faces many difficult situations in his fourth year at Hogwarts. The chart shows some of the ways Harry gets through different events. Complete the chart by giving an example of when each way works for him.

How He Does It	Example From Book
1. Stands up to someone	
2. Uses someone's weakness	
3. Makes plans	
4. Lucky timing	
5. Practices and learns	
6. Asks for advice	
7. Uses magic	

Scholastic Literature Guide • Harry Potter and the Goblet of Fire © 2000 J.K. Rowling. All rights reserved.

Name: _____

Up and Down

Harry feels both happy and sad at different times in this book. Read each statement and decide if he feels "up" or "down." Make a "+" or "–" next to each sentence. Then plot the sentences on the graph and connect the dots. The first two sentences have been done for you.

– 1. Harry has a bad dream and wakes up with his scar hurting.

+ 2. He convinces Uncle Vernon to let him go to the World Cup.

____ 3. No one believes that Harry didn't put his name in the Goblet of Fire.

____ 4. Ron is jealous of him and won't talk to him.

____ 5. Harry tells Cedric about the dragon task.

____ 6. Harry gets past the dragon unscathed.

____ 7. Cho Chang can't go to the ball with Harry.

____ 8. Hagrid is defamed in Rita Skeeter's article.

____ 9. Harry gets points for moral fiber after the second task.

____ 10. Mrs. Weasley and Bill come as his family to watch Harry during the third task.

____ 11. Harry is tied up around Mr. Riddle's gravestone.

____ 12. Dumbledore toasts Harry for his bravery.

		1	2	3	4	5	6	7	8	9	10	11	12
Good +	Very Good		●										
	Good												
	Pretty Good												
Bad –	Pretty Bad	●											
	Bad												
	Very Bad												

Scholastic Literature Guide • Harry Potter and the Goblet of Fire © 2000 J.K. Rowling. All rights reserved.